Saudades do Brasil

Claude Lévi-Strauss

SAUDADES DO BRASIL

A Photographic Memoir

Translated from the French by Sylvia Modelski

UNIVERSITY OF WASHINGTON PRESS *Seattle & London*

NOTE

Saudades do Brasil ("Nostalgia for Brazil") was composed by Darius Milhaud in 1921, at a time when his duties at the French Embassy in Brazil brought him into contact with the popular folk art of this country that he loved and wished to evoke freely.

The author and the publisher of the original edition wish to thank Mme. Madeleine Milhaud, as well as Eschig, the publisher of *Saudades do Brasil*, for giving them permission to use this title.

Originally published under the title *Saudades do Brasil*, copyright © 1994 by Plon, Paris
English translation copyright © 1995 by the University of Washington Press
Photographs copyright © by Claude Lévi-Strauss
Printed in Hong Kong

Library of Congress Cataloging-in-Publication Data
Lévi-Strauss, Claude.
[Saudades do Brasil. English]
Saudades do Brasil : a photographic memoir / Claude Lévi-Strauss ;
translated from the French by Sylvia Modelski.
p.   cm.
ISBN 0-295-97472-9 (alk. paper)
1. Brazil — Pictorial works.   2. Indians of South America — Brazil — Pictorial works.
3. Brazil — Description and travel.   I. Modelski, Sylvia.   II. Title.
F2515.L48913   1995
981 — dc20   95-21579
                                                         CIP

Saudades do Brasil: A Photographic Memoir is published with the assistance of a grant from the University of Washington Press Editor's Endowment, established by Janet and John Creighton and Patti Knowles.

CONTENTS

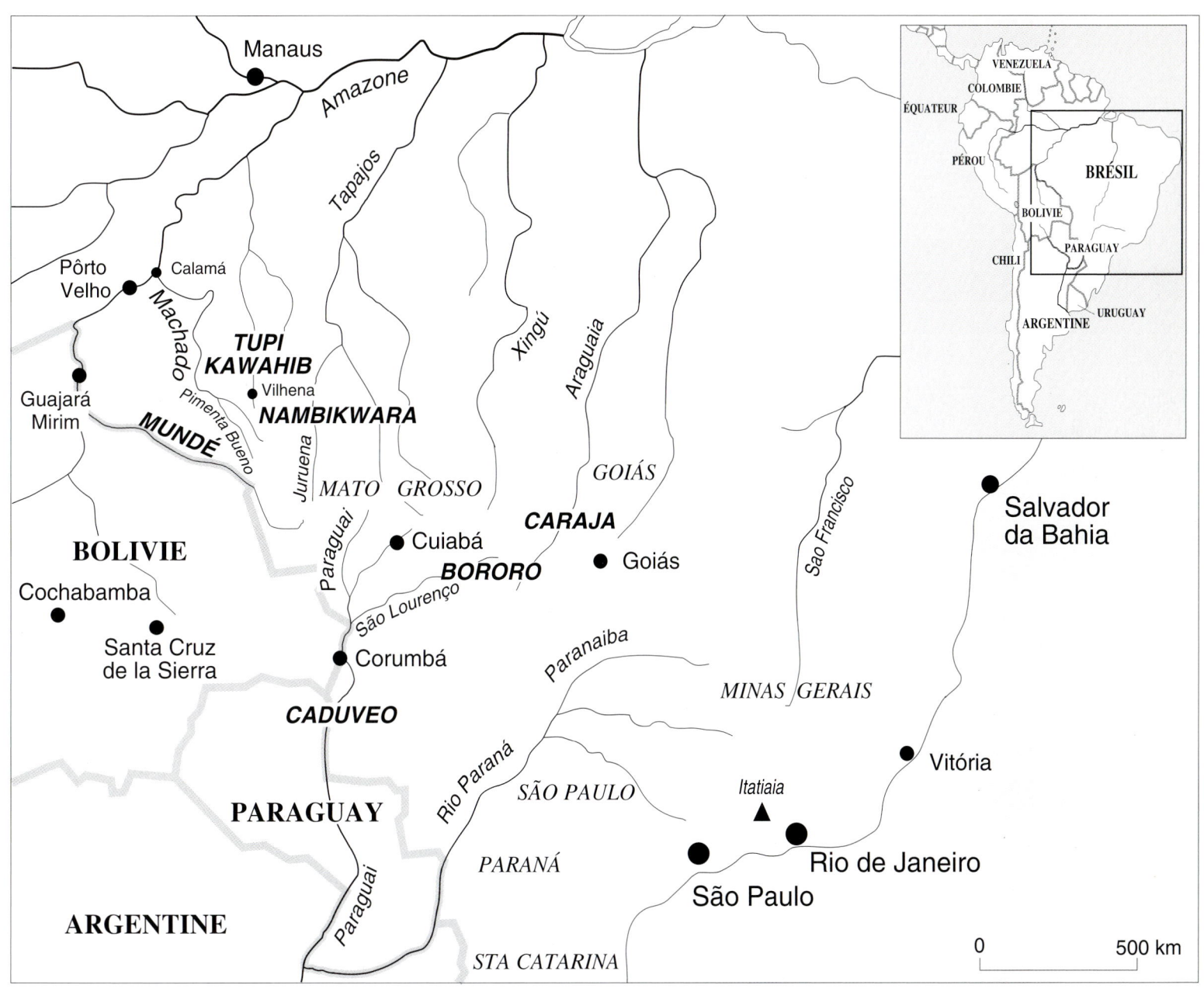

Peoples and places visited by Claude Lévi-Strauss between 1935 and 1939.

PROLOGUE

When I barely open my notebooks, I still smell the creosote with which, before setting off on an expedition, I used to saturate my canteens to protect them from termites and mildew. Almost undetectable after more than half a century, this trace instantly brings back to me the savannas and forests of Central Brazil, inseparably bound with other smells — human, animal, and vegetable — as well as with sounds and colors. For as faint as it now is, this odor — which for me is a perfume — is the thing itself, still a real part of what I have experienced.

Is it because too many years have elapsed (the same number of years for both, though) that photography does not bring any of that back to me? My negatives are not a miraculously preserved, tangible part of experiences that once engaged all my senses, my physical strength, and my brain; they are merely their indices — indices of people, of landscapes, and of events that I am still aware of having seen and known, but after such a long time I no longer always remember where or when. These photographic documents prove to me that they did exist, but they do not evoke them for me or bring them materially back to life.

Upon re-examination, the photographs leave me with the impression of a void, a lack of something the lens is inherently unable to capture. I realize the paradox of offering them again to the public, in greater number, better reproduced, and often displayed differently from what was possible within the format of *Tristes Tropiques*, as if I thought that, in contrast with my own case, the pictures could offer something substantial to readers who have never been there and who therefore must content themselves with this silent imagery, especially since, if they went to see it for themselves, this world would be unrecognizable and would in many respects have simply vanished.

Decimated by smallpox epidemics in 1945 and again in 1975, and reduced in numbers to seven or eight hundred, the Nambikwara today lead a precarious existence close by the religious missions and government posts that watch over the Indians; or else they camp by the side of a road traveled by heavy trucks; or again on the outskirts of the city of 60,000 inhabitants (that was ten years ago; the figure must be higher now) that is rising in the heart of their territory, where in my day the only signs of civilization left after an abortive attempt at penetration were a dozen shanties made of mud-plastered wattle in which a few mixed-blood families languished, dying of hunger and disease.

Nevertheless, it would seem that even quite recently tiny groups of Nambikwara managed to remain, as far as possible, faithful to their traditional life, hunting with bows and arrows in areas not yet invaded by the giant agricultural conglomerates that have taken over the region.

Yet when, in 1992, on the occasion of the five-hundredth anniversary of the discovery of America, representatives of a dozen Amerindian peoples were flown to Mexico City to appear in a movie, the Nambikwara among them were not at all disconcerted by the experience. According to an eyewitness, they arrived equipped with a supply of pamphlets in English, Spanish, and Portuguese denouncing the crimes committed by gold prospectors. They went back home delighted by their trip and bringing with them transistors, which they said were cheaper than those available in Vilhena (the town mentioned above), where the shops are full of Japanese products.

Those about to browse through this collection must be warned against another illusion: the belief that the Indians whom I show completely naked (although it often gets cold at night and in the early morning), sleeping on the ground under makeshift shelters of palm leaves and branches; who produce (and then rarely) only rudimentary pottery and, as for textiles, weave nothing but small decorative items; who cultivate very small gardens between nomadic periods — that these Indians give us an accurate vision of primitive humanity. I myself have never believed this, and over the past twenty years evidence has accumulated to show that the present picture does not reflect archaic conditions. The peoples of Central Brazil and elsewhere are remnants — who have either sought refuge in the interior or been left stranded there — of more advanced and more populous civilizations whose indisputable vestiges are being exhumed or recorded at the mouth and along the whole course of the Amazon by archeologists employing very up-to-date techniques.

When, in 1541, a Spanish expedition that had lost its way sent some fifty men in a boat to look for food, the detachment set off on an unknown river later named the Amazon. After weeks of fruitless navigation that had cut them off from their base, the men, as a last resort, let themselves be carried downstream by the current. They eventually reached a region where, for a distance of 3,000 kilometers, veritable cities appeared before their eyes. According to the expedition's chronicler, Friar Gaspar de Carvajal, each city spread over several leagues along the banks of the river and comprised hundreds of houses of a dazzling whiteness (this notation recurs like a leitmotif, indicating that these were not simply huts). A very dense population lived here, apparently organized into many great chiefdoms, some allied, others hostile, judging from the fortifications adorned with monumental sculptures and the fortresses built on the heights. Well-maintained roads, planted with fruit trees, crossed cultivated fields. They went great distances to who knows what other inhabited centers. The raids the Spaniards made, at some cost to themselves, in order to survive yielded, when successful, huge reserves of food, each sufficient to feed "a troop of one thousand men for a year."

Exactly one century later, an expedition a thousand strong, with a few dozen ships, went (again for the first time) up the Amazon with the express mission of eliminating all the Indians. According to one member of the expedition, they were so numerous that an arrow shot at random into the air was sure to fall back onto somebody's head.

These eyewitness accounts (as well as others that corroborate and complete them) were, if not ignored by historians and anthropologists, at least looked upon with suspicion. It was more convenient, and more soothing for the European conscience, to treat them as exaggerations ascribable to the naiveté or boastfulness of adventurers than to gauge the extent of the massacres by these reports. By the time the voyages of scientific exploration and ethnographic research began in the nineteenth century, the illusion was firmly established that the condition of the Indian communities at that time was the same as it had been in the age of discovery. Travelers and scientists endorsed it.

In the last several years, archeological research has validated the original observations. At the mouth of the Amazon, the island of Marajo, 50,000 square kilometers in area, reveals a multitude of artificial hills, each occupying up to several hectares. They are man-made, erected for defense and to protect the inhabitants and cultivated fields from flooding. On the lower Amazon, remains have been unearthed of cities where, apparently, several tens of thousands of people once lived, as well as traces of unbaked bricks, substantial fortified constructions, and a network of roads leading to distant regions. Still-discernible differences in types of abode suggest that these societies were strongly hierarchical. Based on these data, it is estimated that the population of the Amazon basin was once seven or eight million.

These investigations also show that human occupation of Amazonia dates from much earlier times than the tenth millennium. Need we recall that many archeologists in the United States still subscribe to the dogma that this was the millennium when human beings crossed the Bering Strait and set foot in America for the first time? Yet here and there in the Southern Hemisphere, and more specifically in Brazil, settlements far more ancient than that, on the order of thirty to forty thousand years, have been ascertained by carbon-14 dating. Some of these are arguable, but there is no doubt that thinking about the peopling of America is undergoing radical change.

In Marajo and on the lower Amazon, superbly polished stone objects, and painted ceramics decorated with molded designs whose existence had long been known, were attributed to the influence of Andean civilizations. The belief was that this art would have degenerated when it reached the moist tropical forest environment, with its scant animal and plant resources and a soil and climate that discouraged human settlement. This shows a lack of appreciation of the agricultural potential of the alluvial plains along the river and streams and, above all, of the fact — proven by botanists working on the ground and shown in aerial photographs — that the Amazon forest is not as "primeval" as people liked to think. In many places, the forest reclaimed the land only after the Indians who had cleared and cultivated it were exterminated or pushed to the high ground between the valleys.

Recently, archeological digs have uncovered artifacts that antedate, perhaps by several thousand years, the oldest ceramics from Peru and Ecuador, where it was believed that this art had originated. If there was influence, therefore, it must have been in the opposite direction: Amazonia could be the cradle from which Andean civilizations have sprung.

It is often said that imported diseases, more than massacres, were responsible for the demographic collapse that followed discovery. This may be true in many cases, but it cannot erase the fact that, from the Atlantic to the Amazon, the Portuguese committed a monstrous genocide. It began in the sixteenth century and continued uninterrupted through the eighteenth and nineteenth centuries, the work, principally, of the *bandeirantes*, adventurers in the service of government agencies and of colonists, who used the most horrible methods to reduce the Indians to a state of slavery or simply to destroy them. After the *bandeirantes* came the rubber companies, followed by the real-estate developers who, until a few years ago, took their clients on aerial surveys of vast territories which they promised to deliver *limpiados*, "cleansed" (meaning, of all indigenous presence): today they have been succeeded by gold and diamond prospectors.

One would have to go back to archeological levels from the third millennium B.C. to find a way of life comparable to that of today's Indians. Is it imaginable that they would remain stagnant for four or five thousand years, while in Amazonia itself the lifestyles evolved, in the course of the first millennium B.C., toward a complex political organization and an agricultural economy based mainly on corn?

Not only in Amazonia, but also in its periphery — in Bolivia, in Colombia — aerial photographs have revealed the vestiges of advanced agricultural systems dating from the first centuries of our era. Over tens, at times hundreds, of thousands of hectares of floodland, man-made embankments several hundred meters long and separated by drainage canals, guaranteed year-round irrigation while protecting fields from rising floodwater. Here the Indians practiced an intensive type of agriculture based on tubers which, combined with fishing in the canals, could support more than a thousand inhabitants per square kilometer.

Far from being primitives, the Indians (as they have become known since the study of them began in the last century) survive as the wreckage of these prior civilizations. As early as 1952, I asserted that the Nambikwara were regressive. This is even more obvious with the Caduveo. Numbering about one thousand, they are the last descendants of the Guaicuru, whose society was complex and stratified, divided among nobles, warriors, and slaves. For a long time now, the Caduveo have lived like Brazilian peasants. In the middle of the nineteenth century, however, they were still close enough to their bellicose past to bring decisive aid to the Brazilian army against Paraguay. In gratitude for this, Emperor Pedro II granted them an extensive reserve that, despite the infringements of cattle ranchers, they have succeeded in keeping.

The Bororo fell victim, by the thousands, to the attacks of eighteenth-century adventurers who, organized in bands, rushed headlong into their gold-rich territory. Since the last century, their villages have shrunk to a skeletal state, reduced to a single incomplete circle of huts, where they had once been arranged in a succession of concentric circles around a central area on which might have stood several men's houses, instead of the single one seen today. Only such a high population can explain the extreme complexity of the social organization of the Bororo and of their neighbors who speak the Ge language. It is inconceivable that such a social organization would have been elaborated and applied by populations as small as those that survived into the nineteenth century and the first half of our own. The analogies are so great between this social structure — strikingly reflected in the way the villages are planned — and that of ancient Peru, where Cuzco and the country itself were similarly structured, that the high Andean cultures can no longer be opposed (as was done in the past) to those of the tropical lowlands. There is no doubt that in a very distant past, of which we know almost nothing, there was a continuum between them.

In those who, among the Indians, strike us as being most destitute, we must therefore see not examples of archaic ways of life that have been miraculously preserved for millennia, but the last escapees from the cataclysm that discovery and subsequent invasions had been for their ancestors. Imagine, keeping everything in proportion, scattered groups of survivors after an atomic holocaust on a planetary scale, or a collision with a meteorite such as the one that, they say, caused the extinction of the dinosaurs. The wonder is that with their numbers reduced to the twentieth, the fiftieth, or the hundredth part, these Indians still managed to recreate viable societies and even, it can be said, reinvented the condition for society. Because, fragile as they were, their societies had stability. Demographic stability first of all. Whether deliberate or not, the rules of marriage and certain practices regulating procreation and child care, which we would characterize as superstitious, had the effect of maintaining the population at a level below which it would become extinct, and above which wisdom would require that the group split up. Next, ecological stability, the result of a natural philosophy that subordinates human exploitation of animal and plant resources to respect for a pact concluded with supernatural powers.

Before our eyes, a new cataclysm is dispossessing the Indians of this way of life which they had succeeded in keeping almost intact for one or two centuries. It is caused by the development of communications and the population explosion whose repercussion they suffer at the local level when hordes of adventurers invade the last enclaves where they had found refuge. How can my old photographs fail to create in me a feeling of emptiness and sorrow? They make me acutely aware that this second deprivation will be final this time, given the contrast between a past I still had the joy of knowing and a present of which I receive heartbreaking accounts from sometimes unknown correspondents.

I have already made this point concerning the Nambikwara. The Bororo, whose good health and robustness I had admired in 1935, are today being consumed by alcoholism and disease and are progressively losing their language. It is in missionary schools (which, by a curious reversal, have become the conservators of a culture they had in the first place worked at suppressing, and not without success) that Bororo youths are being taught about their myths and their ceremonies. But, for fear that they might damage the feather diadems, masterpieces of traditional art, the missionaries are keeping these objects locked up, entrusting the Indians with them only on strictly necessary occasions. They would be increasingly difficult to replace since the macaws, parrots, and other brightly colored birds are also disappearing . . .

Far away, in Canada, a contrasting yet strikingly parallel phenomenon is taking place. The Pacific Coast Indians, whom I visited in 1974, are placing in museums — in this case of their own creation — the masks and other ritual objects that were confiscated more than half a century ago and have now been returned to them at last. These objects are brought out and used during ceremonies the Indians are beginning to celebrate again. In this new climate they have lost a good deal of their ancient grandeur. The potlatch, formerly a solemn occasion at once political, juridical, economic, and religious, on which rested the whole social order, has been rethought by acculturated Indians imbued with the Protestant ethic and is degenerating into a periodic exchange of little gifts to consolidate harmony within the group and to maintain friendship. Symbol: displayed next to traditional masks, some of which are among the highest creations of world sculpture, a mask of Mickey Mouse can sometimes be seen, whether made of papier-mâché or molded plastic I do not know.

Why be surprised? When these Indians speak feelingly of their traditional life, they are not thinking of what had already been nothing but a memory for their great-grandparents. The "good old days" for the latter's irremediably acculturated descendants is the period before the Second World War, before 1950 even, when their fishing and gathering economy had not yet been destroyed by regulations protecting natural resources plundered not by them, but by the big timber operations, commercial fishing, and organized tourism . . .

This warped vision of the past is not a purely exotic phenomenon, the unique property of small cultures on the way to extinction. To be convinced of that, one has only to consider what Europe was less than a century ago and what it has become today.

Like most of my contemporaries, I did not realize in 1935 the magnitude of the cataclysm (this one of internal origin) that Europe had had the folly to unleash twenty-one years earlier with the First World War and that would doom it to decline. Its power seemed still intact, its moral domination over the rest of the world unquestioned. It was to the defense of unfortunate exotic cultures menaced by Western expansion that my anthropological colleagues and I thought we should dedicate ourselves.

Things have changed a great deal since then. The victim of circumstances of its own making, Western civilization now feels threatened in its turn. It has, in the past, destroyed innumerable cultures in whose diversity lay the wealth of humankind. Guardian of its own fraction of this collective wealth, weakened by dangers from without and within, it is allowing itself to forget or destroy its own heritage, which — as much as any other — deserves to be cherished and respected.

The population explosion, for which the West shares the responsibility, is reducing the living space between humans at an alarming rate. As for progress, it is devouring itself. More and more, the advances of science and technology, including medical breakthroughs — a blessing for individuals, an evil for our species — have as their principal objective, often used as a pretext, the correction of the harmful consequences of previous innovations. And when that end is achieved, further ill-fated consequences will result, for which it will be necessary to devise other inventions as a remedy. Dispossessed of our culture, stripped of values that we cherished — the purity of water and air,* the charms of nature,

*Speaking to young colleagues and students at the University of São Paulo in 1985, I mentioned the very special quality of the air, a combination of the high altitude and the tropical latitude, which I had recognized as I stepped out of the plane. The whole audience burst out laughing at this, as if I had said something incongruous. Nevertheless, this quality was still present, far from the city; but my audience, plunged daily into the São Paulo inferno, did not identify it as such. They were unable to conceive that an already urbanized existence could be carried on in a still-unpolluted atmosphere.

the diversity of animals and plants — we are all Indians henceforth, making of ourselves what we made of them.

No longer as an anthropologist, but as a member of my civilization, I feel this dispossession profoundly when I look at the pictures of the São Paulo of sixty years ago. I would undoubtedly feel the same looking at photographs of Paris, New York, or Tokyo. But to have seen the city on two occasions, with an interval of half a century in between, makes the shock infinitely more brutal. And São Paulo is an even better example because the changes already under way when I lived there have continued at an accelerated rhythm. From 35,000 inhabitants around 1890, the city's population rose to 340,000 in 1910, reached a million in 1930, and today is twelve or fifteen times that.

In 1935, the city center included two hills linked by a bridge, the *viaduto do Chá*, or "Tea Viaduct," so called because of the plantations that used to occupy the land when it was constructed at the end of the nineteenth century. An English-style public garden, planted with palm trees, was laid out beneath it. When I revisited them in 1985, both the bridge and the park seemed deprived of sunlight, trapped at the bottom of a well. The same suffocating sensation had seized me when crossing the Nihonbashi in Tokyo, which I had imagined as it was 150 years ago — made of wood and dominating the low houses on each side — as in the first woodcut of Hiroshige's *Fifty-three Stages of the Tōkaidō* (or, better still, in Eisen's print in the Kisokaidō series).

When I was living in São Paulo there were, of course, a few tall buildings to be seen here and there, most of them under construction. Only one, still unfinished, towered above the rest. Its architectural style had nothing modern about it. Save for its candy-pink color, it recalled the pre-1914 New York skyscrapers. Despite these relative novelties, the city's history could be seen in clearly visible layers. Civic or religious edifices of the colonial era, long streets lined with shops or dwellings, all of them one-storied and tinted in soft hues. Later, office buildings and commercial establishments dating from the end of the nineteenth century or from around the First World War. These old São Paulo districts, of mixed periods, rose in tiers between ravines that were still left to run wild all the way down to the formerly marshy flats through which the Tietê River meandered. On the highest ground ran the Avenida Paulista, a near equivalent of what the Avenue du Bois must have been in the Paris of the Second Empire. It was lined on both sides by *palacetes*, the mansions of the richest families, already outdated because on the other, southern slope luxurious housing developments called *jardims*, or "gardens," were proliferating, their sinuous avenues serving Spanish-California–style residences that nestled in the greenery.

I myself was renting a place overlooking the city, in a more modest quarter, below the eastern end of the Avenida Paulista, a one-story house of a "modern style" that I would later rediscover in the petit-bourgeois streets of Rome. This style had left its mark as far away as the towns of central Brazil, doubtless the work of Italian immigrant masons (at the time of my stay, half the population of São Paulo was Italian or of Italian descent).

Situated on Rua Cincinato-Braga, my house was part of an old development consisting of twelve dwellings, all alike except that they were built in twin units, each with symmetrical plans. One entered through an iron gate (mine was framed by a thick jasmine) into a small enclosed garden whose walls extended to the back. My yard had two or three palm trees, a carambola, and a medlar tree. I added a banana tree, and there I would take out for an airing my parrots and my capuchin monkey, brought back from my first travels in the interior.

One descended by way of the suburban-looking Avenida Brigadeiro-Luis-Antonio to the city center, the famous commercial and business triangle that bordered upon the oldest part of São Paulo. In 1985, in the course of a lightning visit arranged by a program not under my control, I wished to see again not my house, which must surely have been destroyed, but at least the street. It proved impossible to get to it, however, in the course of my only free morning. I was held back by traffic jams (daily occurrences, I am told) in the Avenida Paulista, now confined between two walls of high-rises. A clearing allowed me to get just a glimpse of an ocean of other high-rises to the south where, in the old days, the *jardims* (Paulista, Europa, America) had offered a charmed life to the well-to-do.

The still half-colonial city I had known, whose population had reached just one million, is today part of an urban conglomeration of twenty-two million. I recently read in a Brazilian journal that, along the east-west axis, one can now drive 170 kilometers without using a highway, only streets. But when I arrived there in the early days of 1939, coming from the Nambikwara with two monkeys, my companions of fortune, the Esplanada, then the most luxurious hotel in the city, made no difficulty at all — not even one remark — in giving us a room where I settled down with my menagerie. In those days in Brazil, still not far removed from the days of Jules Verne, São Paulo had not yet completely lost the memory of its pioneering past. Moreover, the virgin forest was still in evidence on the slopes of the plateau that dropped abruptly to the sea only a few tens of kilometers away. In 1935, the shops still carried maps less than twenty years old where the whole western portion of the state was left blank, with this terse notation: "unknown territories inhabited by the Indians."

I do not claim to be a photographer, not even an amateur (or rather I was not one until Brazil; I no longer have the interest). By contrast my father, who was a portrait painter, had the habit of photographing his subjects to guide him in the placement of their principal features. This procedure had become the common practice among painters since the middle of the nineteenth century. My father took his own photographs, developed them, and printed them himself. From childhood, I became familiar with these operations.

My parents joined me in São Paulo in 1935. At that time the Leica, which had become available commercially a decade earlier, was very popular. My father and I bought our supplies at a shop on São Francisco Square, at the bottom of the Avenida Brigadeiro-Luis-Antonio. There a Central European émigré dealt in second-hand cameras and other photographic curiosities (I still have a Hugo-Meyer F1.5, 75 mm lens, practically unusable because of its weight, but with which one took very beautiful portraits). Father and son competed to see who would obtain the sharpest images. I think that was our main criterion for a successful negative, for we never ceased to marvel how such a small format, when enlarged, could produce very precise details.

In the course of my travels I have owned two Leicas in succession, the second an improved model. Photographs 24 x 36 were taken by one or the other. The 6 x 6 photographs were shot with a twin-lens reflex Voigtlander, which I added to my equipment during my second expedition.

On my first expedition I had, in addition to the Leica, an oval-shaped miniature 8 mm camera whose name I have forgotten. I hardly ever used it, feeling guilty if I kept my eye glued to the viewfinder instead of observing and trying to understand what was going on around me. My patience endured only for a few disjointed series, some of them consisting of rather shaky pictures taken from the saddle.

These snatches of film, rediscovered years later in Brazil, were apparently copied to 16 mm. I was unimpressed when I saw them again, not long ago, at the Centre Georges Pompidou, where they were shown along with other relics.

From about three thousand negatives it was necessary to choose. Besides the fact that some of them brought back only vague memories, they are very uneven in quality and interest. I am grateful to my wife for pulling 13 x 18 trial proofs out of the total lot — a long and thankless task. This allowed a preliminary choice, followed by several others. Some pictures, though mediocre, were included to fill in gaps. Matthieu Lévi-Strauss, whose decisions were critical and who made all the 18 x 24 prints, is, on both these accounts, the coauthor of this book.

The 180 photographs gathered here all relate to South America. In *Tristes Tropiques* India, Pakistan, and what has become Bangladesh also had a place. But I had to leave them out so as not to overburden this collection and to avoid disparity. Let it then be taken for what it is: a testimonial, perhaps not devoid of interest for the historian, to Brazil and its people more than half a century ago, to whom — as well as to my distant youth — I address a friendly and nostalgic salute.

First Looks at Brazil

In 1935 the city of São Paulo, still a frontier town, was visibly turning into an industrial and financial metropolis. Changing from day to day, it offered a fascinating spectacle to the geographer, the sociologist, the anthropologist.

The city also had a singular beauty, due to breaks in rhythm, architectural paradoxes, contrasting shapes and colors. Despite, or perhaps because of, lack of planning, the urban landscape could be lyrical.

The "Tea Viaduct" straddles a park that occupies the bottom of a valley. Clustered around its east side were the Town Hall, the Hotel Esplanada (the most luxurious hotel at the time), the two theaters, the Automobile Club, and the headquarters of important corporations.

On its west side, the viaduct connected the traditional business center, called the "Triangle," and (above) a modern quarter catering to a more elegant trade.

A few hundred meters uphill, modest little gardens dotted ravines where nature still had the upper hand.

From one corner of the Triangle started the Avenida São-João (photographed on a carnival day), dominated by the pink mass of the then incomplete Predio Martinelli. In 1985 I saw it again in its completed state, hemmed in on all sides by other office towers.

East of the Avenida Paulista fashionable residences abruptly gave way to decaying districts.

Behind the imposing buildings, street-level shops painted in various colors lined the old streets.

In midtown, cattle compete for the road with the trolley car, always jammed during rush hour.

My father takes a picture in front of our house on Cincinato-Braga. For me, the not too outdated Ford was a symbol of social success, since in France I had owned a mere Citroën 5 CV three-seater, also acquired second-hand.

About 50 kilometers northwest of São Paulo, Pirapora do Bom Jesus, its houses reflected in the waters of the Tietê River, seemed to belong to the colonial era.

A place of pilgrimage, the village experienced periodic bursts of excitement. Mule drivers coming from miles around camped on the outskirts.

A predominantly black crowd thronged the streets.

Groups gathered around people in a trance.

There was a "house of miracles."

The walls of a vast room, about 20 meters long, were covered with ex-voto photographs of people who had been cured by a miracle or of pilgrims soliciting some favor from heaven.

This picture was probably taken in August 1937, around the fifteenth of the month.
An angel idles in front of the stalls while waiting for the procession.

The trip took place in early September 1937, at first by car on roads that deteriorated rapidly, then on horseback, finally on foot. Martonne is on the left.

A glimpse of Martonne's legs in the chimney
leading to the summit.

Then Martonne (seen here between a young Brazilian geographer on the left and René Courtin on the right) gave an impromptu lecture that to me, because of my literary training, seemed a wonderful textual criticism. I realized that a landscape, when looked at and analyzed by a master, can become an exciting reading experience, as capable of training the mind as a commentary on a play by Racine.

Forest fires broke out in the mountains during our climb, making the return trip difficult.

Southwest of the state of São Paulo, largely unexplored at the beginning of this century, the border state of Paraná was being opened to colonization.

Nevertheless, here and there the traditional life persisted. Witness this *caboclo*, the name given to poor peasants of the interior . . .

. . . this file of horses heavy-laden with firewood . . .

. . . this urchin bringing in (and taking a bite out of) a harvest of ears of corn.

Farther into the interior of the state, the virgin forest still occupied immense expanses that we traversed on horseback for several days in order to reach a Kaingang Indian reserve.

A peaceful little fishing village on the coast of the state of Santa Catarina, contiguous to the southern region of the state of Paraná.

The state of Santa Catarina, especially in the coastal towns, is a region of old German colonization going back to the nineteenth century. Hence the success of the *Integralistas*, the Brazilian fascist party whose members wore green shirts with an emblem in the form of a Greek sigma (Σ), instead of a swastika, on the sleeve.

At the end of June or the beginning of July 1937, René Courtin invited Jean Maugüé and me to travel north from São Paulo and go as far as his car would take us. Jean Maugüé has written an account of this trip in his book *Les Dents agacées* ["Teeth Set on Edge"] (Paris: Buchet-Chastel, 1982). I referred to it briefly in *Tristes Tropiques*, chapter 12.

The rapids and falls of the Paranaiba River, which marks the border of the state of Goiás.

We passed
through villages
at long distances
from each other.
It can be seen
that the roads
were little more
than tracks.

Oxcarts, horses, or pack mules were then the common means of transportation in these regions.

The part of the caravansary reserved for people showed, by its architectural refinement, that it had once known a more prosperous time.

Old Goiás, then the state capital, led an uneventful life in the shade of mango trees.

It was then a sleepy town in the heart of a hilly and gracious landscape.

Structures of a pronounced "modern" style, in front of eighteenth-century façades, attested to the passing presence of Italian artisans.

The trail ended, and the expedition came to a halt on the banks of the Araguaia—we could have gone on only by water—next to a few Karaja Indian families that had settled there.

The women made dolls of unbaked clay for their granddaughters. These toys were painted, their heads covered with black wax simulating heavy locks, adorned with multicolored threads, and dressed in a loincloth of beaten bark. Since the advent of tourism, this art has grown tremendously, and not for the better.

*From the Caduveo
to the Bororo*

In the autumn of 1935, instead of returning to France for the summer holidays (which coincided with the northern winter), my first wife and I left for the Mato Grosso, accompanied by a French friend who had come to join us. The aim was to visit the Caduveo and Bororo Indians and bring back ethnographic collections for the Musée de l'Homme, after giving the required share to Brazil.

Pulled by a wood-burning locomotive, our train reached the terminus of the line on the Paraguay River in three days. It took us three more days on horseback to get to the Caduveo villages.

Caduveo designs.

At the border between Brazil and Paraguay, the Pantanal, the largest marshland in the world, isolates the Caduveo.

The villages are situated on top of small hillocks for protection against flooding.

Aside from language, it is facial paintings that, in the eyes of the uninformed visitor, distinguish these Indians from Brazilian peasants. Occasionally, mainly in play, they may be drawn on the face of a little boy.

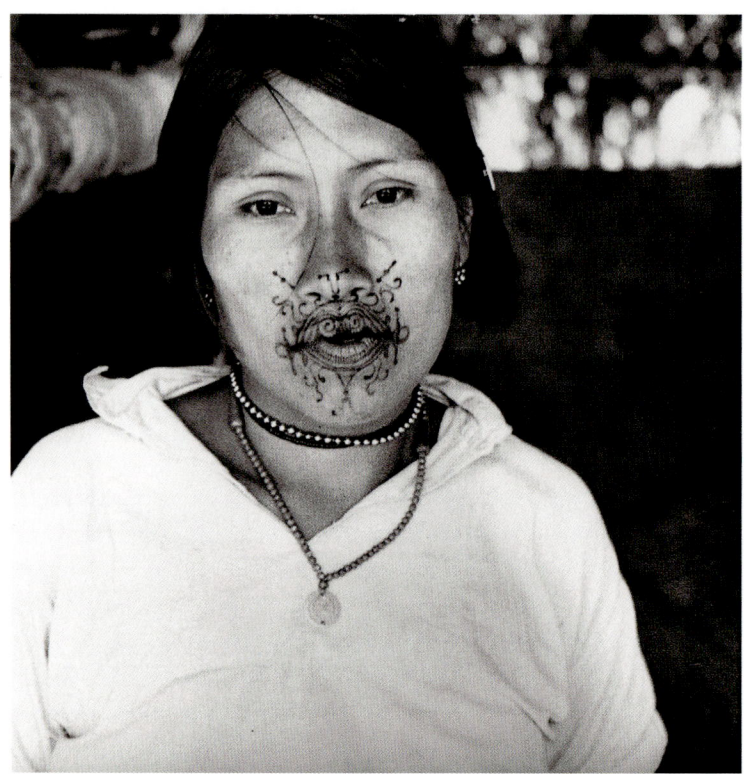

Traditionally, facial paintings were reserved for the women, who perform this service for each other.

The mouth becomes a strange and complicated flower . . .

. . . or the whole face, crossed by a vertical design of S's, is divided into geometric sectors.

Old women, extraordinary virtuosos, adorned with jewelry made of hammered pieces of silver . . .

. . . invent designs so free that they almost ignore the features of the human face.

When wood for the boiler or meat became scarce, we replenished our supplies from a peasant who lived not too far from the shore.

The boat at the port of Cuiabá.

Nearby, a bath for the horses.

Stock farms scattered in the near vicinity supplied the *saladeiros*, where meat, first salted then dried—the staple diet, with rice and black beans, of the interior—was prepared . . .

. . . under the greedy eyes of vultures.

Cuiabá, capital of the state of Mato Grosso, was founded at the beginning of the eighteenth century on land rich in gold.

Several days' journey by truck took us to the São Lourenço River, a tributary of the Cuiabá River. To reach Bororo villages not yet controlled by the missions, we had to go upstream by canoe. With a few fishermen, hired to take us there, we claimed our daily meal from the river.

One day we killed a 7-meter female water boa that was about to give birth.

Perched on the roof of a cabin like the macaws the Indians bred for their plumage,
I took a panoramic view of the unchanging structure of Bororo villages: the men's
house in the center and family dwellings, owned by the women, in a circle around it.
An invisible line of demarcation cuts across the men's house and divides the village
into two halves. A man born in one half must choose a wife from the other half, and
vice versa.

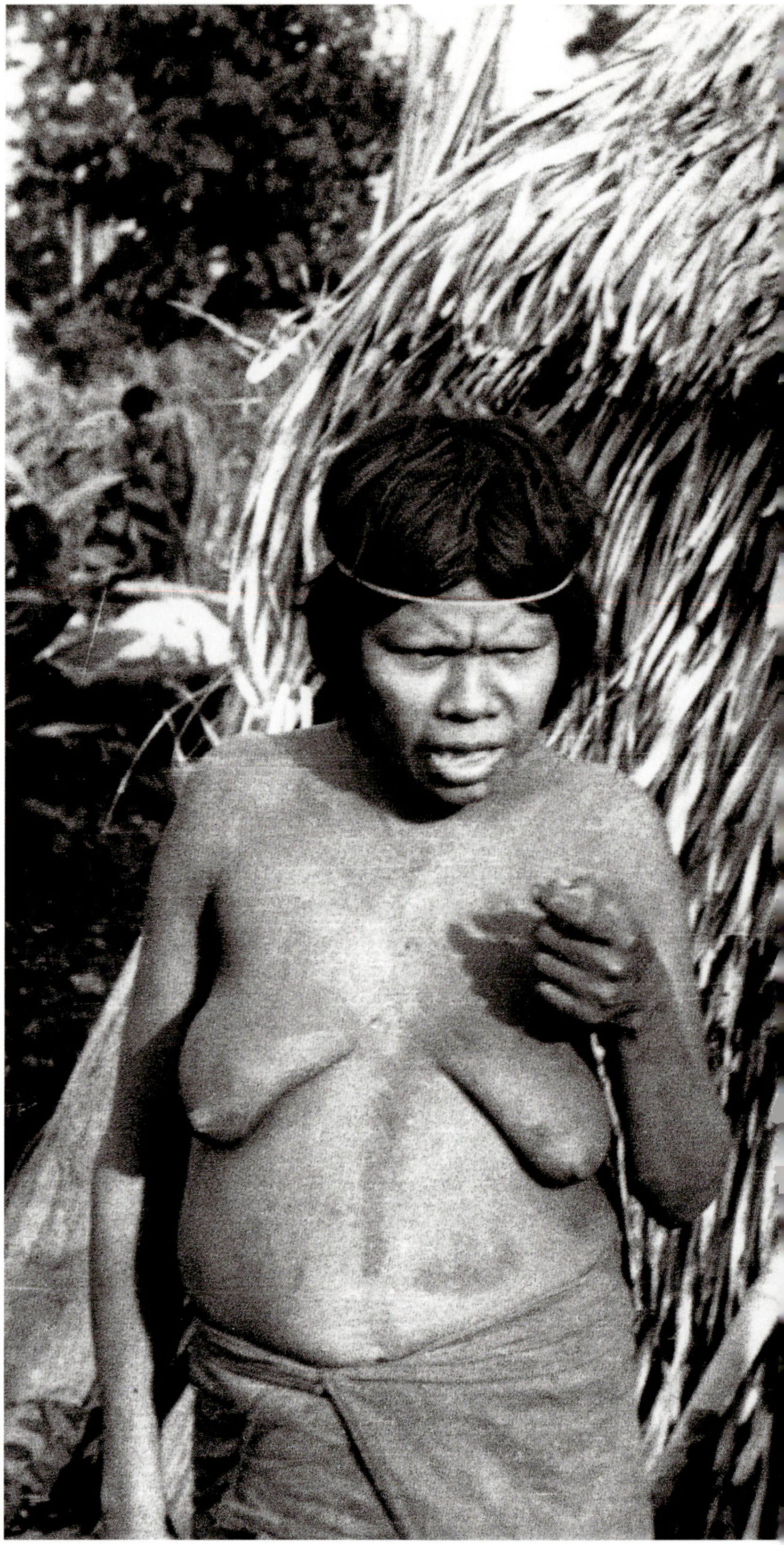

With no other opening except a small door cut out of the straw partition, the family cabins are always dark; the only light they receive is what filters in between the palm leaves. Bed frames covered with matting are the only furniture.

In their daily lives men and women
dressed simply . . .

. . . for men limited to the wearing of a penis sheath, seen here on the crouching Indian facing the camera.

In anticipation of a feast, however, this sheath was decorated with a mosaic of feathers and a streamer of straw, emblazoned with the distinctive symbol of the wearer's clan.

94   *From the Caduveo to the Bororo*

Raised by missionaries and even, he claimed, taken to Rome and presented to the Pope, this man—his hair dyed with red stain from the annatto tree—spoke a little Portuguese. Returned to his village to lead a traditional life, faithful to the old customs, he was a valuable informant.

On festive occasions and at ceremonies, the women adorned themselves with all their finery: bandoleers of beads, pendants of animal teeth. The woman in front holds a fan.

For their part, the men arrayed themselves in sumptuous finery: down tufts glued with resin, a feather diadem, a labret of articulated mother-of-pearl elements, a pendant of giant armadillo claws, an emblazoned bow.

At dusk, one part of the population sat down to watch the dance spectacle offered by the other part.

Funeral ceremonies in honor of an Indian who had died away from the village last for several days . . .

. . . in the course of which the "souls" of the dead come back to visit the living.

Secular festivities are interspersed among these religious rites. The strongest men compete . . .

. . . to see who can lift and carry for the longest time huge disks . . .

. . . one said to be "male" and the other "female"; these were made of segments of palm stalks held together by straw bindings and rolled up like a long and narrow rope ladder.

These joyful exercises are the Bororo variant of races held by other peoples of central and eastern Brazil, in which the competitors carry heavy logs.

The World of the
Nambikwara

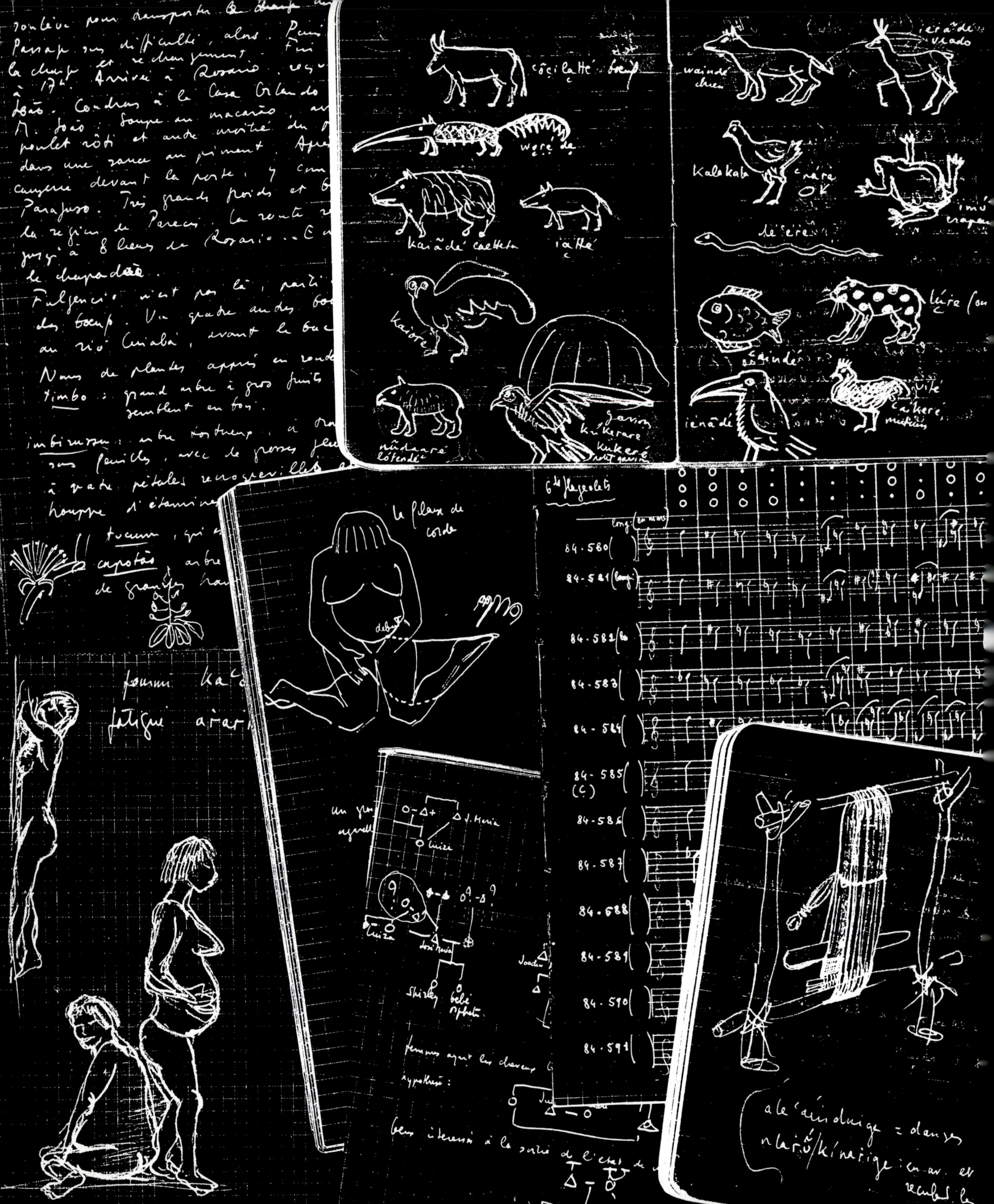

About sixty years ago, the most perilous part of an expedition to the interior of Brazil was surely the part attempted by car or truck. Trails that were barely cleared or were traced by the wheels of infrequent traffic served as roads. Every day, and often several times a day, the truck nearly overturned; or else it got mired, stuck in sand, or immobilized in a bog or in front of an obstacle that could be surmounted only by maneuvering several jacks at the same time. The slowness of the operations made it necessary to camp in the bush.

110   Streams were crossed on fragile bridges that every user had to repair before venturing on them.

The same was true for getting across larger rivers on primitive ferries that were sometimes too short and that threatened to sink under the weight of even an empty truck.

It could take a whole day to unload the truck, transfer to the other side the equipment, provisions, and cans of gasoline necessary for the trip there and back, get the truck across, and then reload it.

Once my truck was stranded nearly a week by a mechanical breakdown. It blocked the way at the top of a very rugged hill and, as luck would have it, a Syrian or Lebanese peddler, carrying supplies to a distant station and also driving a truck, arrived at the same place. For him to get past, a new trail had to be opened by splitting the rocks with a sledgehammer.

In the meantime, my troop of draft oxen, horses, and pack mules, led by about fifteen men, was making its way at an even more leisurely pace.

Henceforth, the journey would continue on horseback in arid and rugged country that the maps had long called Serra do Norte, although it does not have any mountains.

The trail, which could hardly be called fit for vehicles, ended at the edge of the Papagaio River, a tributary of the Amazon. On the last ferry we met the Nambikwara, who use it willingly.

I knew the Nambikwara in the dry season, during a period of nomadic existence. At such times they live under flimsy shelters made of palm fronds stuck into the sandy soil.

The Nambikwara sleep on the ground—an unusual custom among the South American
Indians, who invented the hammock.

Their diet consisted of thick manioc pancakes cooked under ashes . . .

. . . and game—rare in this season—such as, on this day, four toucans.

Craftsmanship under the shelter: this woman pierces a shell fragment from which she makes an ornament.

Here one can make out the partly hidden figure of a man weaving a narrow band on a small, improvised loom.

The preparation of curare for hunting arrows: filtering a decoction of strychnos roots.

The liquid is then heated until thick. The leaf in the man's hand is used to taste the brew and evaluate its consistency and strength.

The villagers bathed upon awakening as well as at other times of the day, here in the company of the anthropologist.

The men hold archery competitions just for the fun of it (the arrow in the foreground, with a blunt tip, is used to hunt birds without damaging their feathers).

A team sport is played with a ball of wild rubber in a clearing that accurately conveys the desolate character of some parts of the region.

An epidemic of very painful, suppurating eye inflammation struck the Indians while we were there. Several members of the expedition were contaminated. We witnessed some distressing scenes.

The Indians treated each other with liquid instillations (whose nature I was not able to ascertain) from a leaf that was rolled into a cone to act as an eyedropper.

Nambikwara men vary greatly in physical type. Some, with a strongly hooked nose and hairy face, contrast with other Indians of Brazil.

A headdress (called "of war") made of jaguar skin.

Feathered nasal ornaments . . .

. . . nasal bars and labrets, made of bamboo fibers, in the upper lip . . .

. . . are changed daily (note the cigarette of tobacco rolled in a dry leaf and stuck into the narrow band tightly clasping the arm).

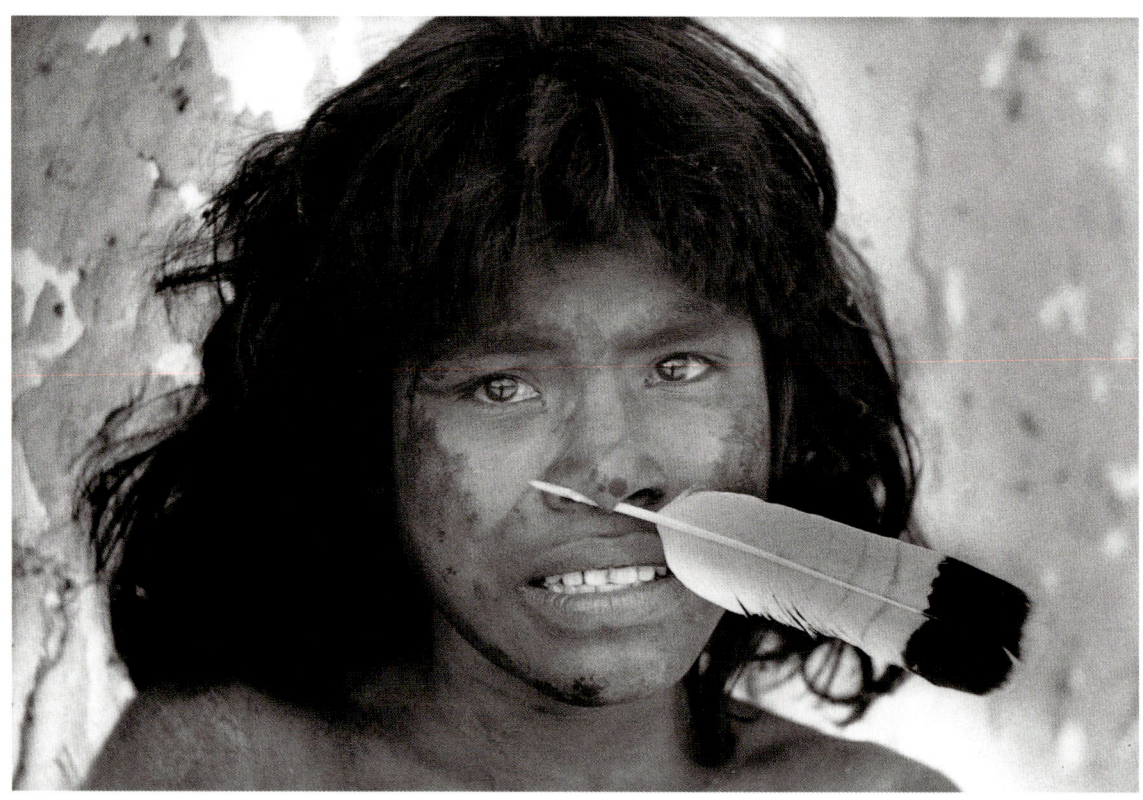

Sometimes the Indians will wake in the morning with blotches of ash on their face. Feeling the dawn chill, they go closer to the fire in their sleep.

Several Nambikwara households are polygamous.

But polygamous or monogamous . . .

. . . they exhibit a joyful affection.

In twos . . .

. . . or indeed in threes, they express tenderness in broad daylight . . .

. . . except in the case of this woman, who seemed marginalized, perhaps because she was still nursing her baby.

She wore no ornaments and lived somewhat apart from the others with her husband and child.

A few Nambikwara had patches of discolored skin. This does not detract anything from the charm of this woman, who holds a puppy close to her body.

The women loved to keep pets—in this case a little capuchin monkey—which they raised like children and which served them as a headdress.

The attractiveness of the Nambikwara, notwithstanding their wicked reputation, is largely explained by the presence in their midst of very young women who were graceful despite their sometimes rather thick waists.

Dreamy when the mood struck them . . .

. . . most often merry . . .

. . . mocking, provocative . . .

. . . they remained aware of their prettiness even during delousing sessions (note the bracelets made of segments of giant armadillo tail).

Delousing was also done in groups.

Nambikwara children, whose play is essentially the imitation of adults, spend their days together.

For the little girls, a puppy serves as a doll and is carried around as an infant is by its mother.

When they are a little older, they will look after a little sister . . .

. . . seen here asleep on the sand.

This young boy wears a feather threaded through his nasal septum and mother-of-pearl earrings . . .

. . . this one wears the labret and the nose pin.

A young capuchin monkey clings to the hair of this crouching little girl.

Another girl digs for an edible root; perched on her head is a small, female, woolly monkey that she will soon give to me in exchange for some coveted object.

The little creature, whom I christened Lucinda, will not leave my side until my departure from Brazil.

I prevailed upon the Nambikwara to lead me to the site of their winter village in order to meet other friendly or allied bands. We followed them on horseback with a few oxen laden with gifts.

We stopped in the evening to camp in the sparsely wooded savanna, typical of the Mata Grosso landscape.

Sometimes these stops were lengthened beyond reason because the Indians, aware that our horses and oxen would not be able to go by their usual route, were not sure of the alternative way they had planned.

This picture and the three preceding ones show how the gasoline cans that had fueled our truck had become an integral part of the personal possessions of the Nambikwara.

The site of the winter village.

A few huts, sturdier than the palm shelters, were the signs of an intermittent occupation. Toward evening, about seventy people, arriving in small groups, assembled.

In Amazonia

To reach them, we had to go by canoe for several days up the Pimenta
Bueno River, a tributary of the Machado River.

The river went deep into a vast forest. Here and there, strange rock formations emerged from the water.

At any moment we were likely to have to unload and carry our gear, and often our canoes, on our backs as we made our way along the river banks . . .

. . . until, with the canoes once more afloat, the passengers were able to re-embark.

We negotiated the rapids through the laborious use of poles.

Our camp, a short distance from the Mundé village.

At Cuiabá, I had commissioned a seamstress to make a mosquito net of my own design for the hammock (it is seen here in the right foreground). It was both comfortable and impenetrable, easy to keep off the ground so that no snake, scorpion, spider, poisonous ant, or other aggressive little creature could enter. In New York, during the war, an American intelligence service (I no longer remember which) grilled me about my travels and had all my negatives printed. The mosquito net interested them very much, and I was asked for its pattern and dimensions.

The Mundé village consisted of three communal huts surrounded by gardens. When the land was cleared, the stumps of the palm trees were left standing at a height of about one meter because the fat white grubs prized as food thrived in them. This is, in a way, the poultry yard.

The huts were artfully constructed.

Each hut housed five or six families.

Young women . . .

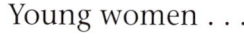

. . . and mature ones had a pronounced taste for adornment. They wore a great deal of jewelry: mother-of-pearl shells, and necklaces, belts, and nose pins made of small beads of black palm nut alternating with white shell.

Great care was lavished on hair: bangs were singed straight with embers, temples depilated by plucking the short hairs with a twisted string, eyelashes and eyebrows removed either by hand or with wax.

The men were equally fastidious in their personal grooming.

On their upper and lower lips they wore labrets of hardened resin, translucent and golden as amber.

One had the impression that this small community, well supplied with animal and vegetable food, lived a life of leisure, principally preoccupied with bodily beauty.

The village itself was like a gem set in the forest.

Unlike the Nambikwara, the Mundé did not smoke. They were not, however, averse to tobacco, like the Tupi-Kawahib. The men blew powdered tobacco into each others' noses through a long tube lengthened at one end by an oblique tip that was inserted into the partner's nostril.

Such details as the position of the hand for drawing a bow, different from that of the Nambikwara, are of interest to the anthropologist.

A too-short visit ends with the exchange of presents. In return for a small crate of iron axheads, machetes, and a bolt of fabric (center), we received (left) bows, arrows, and baskets filled with calabashes decorated with burned-on designs.

Also discovered at the beginning of this century, the Tupi-Kawahib were at one time an important nation made up of friendly and hostile clans. They were thought to have disappeared or to have merged with the local population of rivermen and rubber prospectors. The existence of a small group that had kept its independence was brought to my attention, however, when I was in their area (see *Tristes Tropiques*, chapters 31-34).

A page from the author's notebook

According to the information we had gathered, the village was situated three days by canoe downstream on the right bank of the Machado River. After that we walked for two days through the forest to reach it.

The population consisted of about twenty people divided among four quadrangular houses. In the foreground is the big earthenware basin in which corn is simmered for the manufacture of a lightly fermented beverage called *cahouin*. A harpy eagle's cage is at the back. Like several other tribes, the Tupi-Kawahib keep this powerful raptor in captivity when they succeed in capturing it. Its feathers, striped black and white, are prized above all others, and magical properties are attributed to its flesh and droppings.

A woman brews the *cahouin*.

A hunting accident whose victim was one of my crew forced us to leave the village precipitately. For two weeks, I remained camped by the side of the Machado with the Indians who intended afterward to settle at the station at Pimenta-Bueno.

Ever since she lived in my company, Lucinda (see page 154) had chosen, as her habitual position, to cling to one of my legs.

The Indians spent some of their time hunting. Here, a good-sized coata monkey — also called spider monkey — is being skinned. Like the Mundé, the Tupi-Kawahib wear a penis sheath.

The meat is smoke-cured on a wooden frame called a buccan.

In contrast to the Nambikwara, who avoid using proper names and even keep them secret from strangers, the Tupi-Kawahib use them openly. The village chief was called Taperahi.

Of his four wives, Kunhatsin was the most beautiful.

Another, Maruabai, was Kunhatsin's mother by a previous union.

On the face of the third one, Takwame, can be traced the dark blue tattoo the women wore from the ear to the chin. The women wove the loincloths they used to wear, the carrying bands, and the hammocks.

Ianopamoko, the chief's youngest wife, was lame. She used two sticks to help her walk, which did not prevent her from taking long hikes in the forest with her family.

Pwereza, one of the chief's sons, inspects an old powder flask.

The old bullet casings worn on a necklace by Penhana and other women date perhaps from contacts with the military expedition that discovered the Tupi-Kawahib in 1915.

The Return

As the rivers get wider and deeper,
we graduate from dugout canoes to light craft made of wooden planks.

Pages from the author's notebook.

As soon as the first settlement of rubber prospectors upstream is reached, we can bid farewell to canoes and rowboats.

A motorboat will take us to the Madeira River.

But each time we hit a shallow, the boat has to be lightened by unloading cargo, and trunks, boxes, and bundles must be hauled along the bank.

We no longer disembark every evening to camp by the river. Life goes by entirely on board.

There we cook, there we eat, there we sleep.

To take on balls of crude rubber . . .

. . . we occasionally call on an isolated rubber prospector.

The boat creeps lazily along the meanders . . .

. . . and skirts the islets.

At Calamá, where the Machado flows into the Madeira, a modest steamship plies the river up to the Bolivian border . . .

. . . where I will await the uncertain arrival of a small amphibian.

Still traveling by air, I reach Cochabamba, then Santa Cruz de la Sierra with its austere and old-fashioned streets.

A typical Bolivian market.

After passing through Corumbá, back in Brazil, and then through Cuiabá, I returned by truck to Nambikwara country, where I rejoined my team and the Indians, who were busy erecting a winter hut.

Laden with ethnographic collections, the truck finally returns to Cuiabá (see page 84).

Last glimpses of Brazil: ports of call of the mixed-cargo boat that was taking me back to France.

The harbor of Vitória, north of Rio de Janeiro.

The Pelourinho, upper quarter of Bahia . . .

. . . and its innumerable churches dating from the colonial era.

Many years later, in Amazonian Peru, an American colleague took this photograph of young Cashinaua Indians looking at some of these pictures (photograph by David Allison, used by permission).